BARGELLO

FLORENTINE CANVAS WORK

ELSA S. WILLIAMS

REINHOLD BOOK CORPORATION
NEW YORK / AMSTERDAM / LONDON

This book is dedicated to

June Sundstrom Clark

Published in the United States of America, 1967, by
Reinhold Publishing Corporation
A subsidiary of Chapman-Reinhold, Inc.,
430 Park Avenue, New York, N. Y.
All rights reserved
Library of Congress Catalog Card Number 67-24705
Type set by Graphic Arts Typographers, Inc.
Printed and bound in Tokyo, Japan,
by Zokeisha Publications, Ltd.

Second Printing, 1969

ACKNOWLEDGEMENTS

My sincere appreciation is extended to Claire Peters Schrock for her valuable assistance in working many of the designs shown in this book.

For their cooperation at the Museo Nazionale (Bargello), I wish to thank Professor Luciano Berti, Director of the National Museums of Florence, Italy; and Signor Luigi Giovani, Superintendent of the Bargello. I am especially grateful to Signora Rosalia B. Fanelli, Curator of Textiles, who provided factual information on the original Bargello pieces of canvas work.

Additional research of the designs was made possible by the generous assistance of Miss Sinclair Salmon, Secretary of the Embroiderers' Guild, and Mr. Michael Darby at the Victoria and Albert Museum in London.

My gratitude is also extended to Heinz Edgar Kiewe of Oxford, for his valued opinions and for his own efforts in keeping the art of canvas work alive during the past years.

My thanks also, to Clara Fried Zwiebel who edited this book, and to Mr. George H. Boyer for his excellent black and white photography.

ALPHABETICAL LIST OF PATTERNS

One of the famous Bargello chairs. Photograph by Bertoni. Courtesy of Museo Nazionale, Florence, Italy.

THE STORY OF BARGELLO

All history is interlaced with legends which very often include some mystery. This is especially true with the history of Bargello Embroidery, a stitchery widely known by many other different names.

With my first inquiries about this Florentine canvas work, I heard an intriguing story of a most unusual and philanthropic Italian nobleman who, during the fourteenth century, provided canvas and embroidery thread to the inmates of the Bargello prison in Florence. This was, perhaps, one of the earliest programs of rehabilitation and probably may have been where some of the lovely repeat patterns of the Flame Stitch originated and were developed, as well as some other beautiful canvas embroidery stitches which I have included with my designs in this volume. This was a fascinating thought and often, as I worked an intricate and very difficult design on a piece of canvas, I wondered if the same pattern had not been worked in the past by a clever criminal or a traitor who had been put to death there in the courtyard.

When it was suggested that I write a book about Bargello Embroidery, I decided to go to Florence to learn for myself as much as possible about the actual historical facts. Until now there had only been a few uncertain references to be found on the subject. Spring of 1967 was a sad time in the city and her industrious merchants and businessmen were busy recovering from the terrible effects of the flood caused a few months before by the rampaging River Arno. The Bargello, which is now called the Museo Nazionale, suffered severe damage from water and deep mud. Huge air blowers were operating to attempt to dry out the exhibits on the main floor galleries. The Florentine artisans, with the aid of friends and volunteers from all over the world, were making every effort to restore the precious objects for all to see again. Surely the visit of an American needlewoman must have been unimportant to the directors of the museum in view of the urgency and magnitude of their problems. They were delighted, however, to hear my amusing story of Bargello Embroidery and I soon discovered that they were quick to shatter the fanciful myths.

It is true that the Bargello was the Palace of the Podesta, the sinister and powerful chief magistrate, and it was also a prison. However, it was a political prison where men condemned to die spent their last hours. Since the time they spent in the Bargello was usually short, only a few days before the end, it is unlikely that they had either the time to embroider or the inclination. In addition they were probably handcuffed or chained in dark dungeon cells which certainly was not conducive to producing canvas embroidery.

The Bargello, a very fine specimen of thirteenth-century architecture, became a national museum. It was formally established in 1857 and now houses some of the greatest art treasures of the world. The executions which took place in the courtyard are overshadowed by the great works of Donatello, Verrocchio, Michelangelo, Ghiberti, and the Della Robbias. Included in the textile collection we can find only one pattern of so-called Bargello canvas embroidery. Four seventeenth-century armchairs are to be seen, all worked in the same design with silk threads in shades of green, yellow, white, and dark-blue. According to the museum's inventory of furniture, "Seven chairs, 17th-century, with backs and seats done in *punto unghero* silk embroidery, were purchased by the museum on September 23, 1886, from a Signor Menichetti." Hence, these chairs were bought almost 30 years after the Bargello building was transformed into the Museo Nazionale.

It is especially interesting to notice that the inventory lists the chairs as *punto unghero*, meaning Hungarian Point embroidery, which leads us to a second story about this type of canvas work. This legend is about a Hungarian princess who married an Italian nobleman of the Medici family. Her trousseau is said to have contained many beautiful pieces trimmed with Hungarian Point embroidery and it was she perhaps, who taught the ladies of the Florentine court the art of *punto unghero*. Whether or not this is true cannot be traced today. At the present time only a few pieces of Florentine canvas work of the period remain in Italy and this type of embroidery art does not enjoy any great popularity there.

There is another historical discovery which may, perhaps, give credence to the story of the Hungarian origin and some additional proof of the derivation of this type of canvas work. Maria Undi, in her book on Hungarian Fancy Needlework, writes that "Princess Jadwiga (Hedwig) of Hungary was married in 1383, at the age of 13, to Polish King Vladislav V of the Jagiello family, and took the love of beautiful embroidery with her to her new home. It is recorded that she herself embroidered a bishop's ornate cape, richly embellished with beads, for the cathedral of Cracow. A part of the shoulder ribbon embroidered with the coat-of-arms of Poland at one end and the Hungarian coat-of-arms at the other is still preserved today."

was also a great interest in beautiful decoration and elegant fabrics. The art of embroidery, which had formerly been applied chiefly to religious vestments and ecclisiastical linen and adornment, now burst forth into greater and more diversified use. Italian craftsmen developed excellent dyeing methods and produced colorful silk and wool in hues which harmonized with the paintings and colors of the Renaissance.

In addition to surface embroidery, the Florentine craftsmen worked their beautiful threads into elegant, canvas-based fabrics which could not be produced by weaving looms. Here, perhaps, was the beginning of what we today call Bargello, Florentine Canvas Work, or Hungarian Point.

I do not believe this type of stitchery should be called Flame Stitch. The term is misleading, since it only identifies the particular patterns which are worked in gradations of serrated peaks and slopes. It cannot be classified as Florentine Embroidery alone since Florentine Embroidery would need to include other surface stitchery as well as canvas work. To classify it as *Point dé Hongrie*, which translated means Hungarian Stitch, may also confuse the embroiderer who will accept only the familiar surface embroidery stitch with this same name. Florentine Canvas Work is undoubtedly, then, the most correctly applicable general term.

Since the name Jagiello is also spelled 'Jagello' and there is historic reference to the Jagellon dynasty, it is not unlikely that over the centuries the name Jagiello and Bargello were transposed. When speculating on this possibility, one must remember that the boundaries of European countries varied considerably from those of today and there were many political marriages which merged the families and lands of many rulers. It is, therefore, not at all surprising to find a similarity in the history of needlework which was practised everywhere in Europe during the fourteenth and fifteenth centuries. The ladies of every country took their needlework with them wherever they lived and it is no wonder that we are using the same basic stitches today.

It is interesting to learn that *Point dé Hongrie* was the favorite embroidery of Queen Maria Teresa, in the eighteenth century. Her work, which is preserved at the Hungarian National Museum, establishes her importance in the history of fine needlework.

During the reign of Lorenzo de Medici in the fifteenth century, Florence became the cultural center of the world. Here, where artists created beautiful paintings and sculpture, there

The reader then may well ask why I continue to call this canvas work Bargello, now that I know it is really only an alias. My answer must include the knowledge that it has become an accepted name for generations. Added to this is the fact that when examining the great chairs of the Bargello, it is important to notice that the stitches of these famous pieces create beautiful texture, fascinating color effects, and constant repeat design. They are the masterpieces and prime examples of what can be accomplished with this fascinating stitchery. I realize that the needlework legends of the Bargello are untrue, but I hope that future generations will continue to associate the name with beautiful canvas work.

The exciting effects achieved with Bargello Embroidery depend chiefly upon the careful use of color. The designs in this book are keyed to present-day adaptations of these patterns using colors which will complement modern color schemes. All of the designs may be worked in the needleworker's own choice of colors but the forms are created by cleverly shading the colors. Some patterns require every row to be of a different color and some consist of several shades of the same color, progressing from the lighter to the darker hue and then back again from the dark to the light.

Many old Florentine pieces were worked in silk threads on fine gauze-like canvas. Heavier effects have been achieved using these repeat patterns to make carpets and rugs on coarse, strong, jute canvas using several strands of wool yarn together as one. It is actually possible to work these designs on any evenly woven fabric which will accommodate the chosen thread or yarn to create the overall effect produced by this type of stitching. All the designs shown in this book were worked in soft tapestry wool on 13 thread-to-the-inch mono canvas. For practical application I believe this to be the most effective base for Bargello Embroidery. The size of the stitch is easy to see and the tapestry wools create a beautiful blending of texture and color.

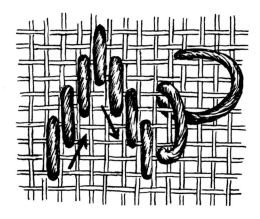

All Bargello stitches are laid lengthwise following the weave of a single-mesh canvas, using flat vertical stitches (not diagonally as is customary with needlepoint). Many simple patterns are worked by continuously stitching over four threads of canvas. Diamond, geometric, and serrated patterns are usually worked over four threads and under two threads in a diagonal movement up and down the canvas as shown in the diagram. These evenly-spaced stitches are delightful to work and they create a beautiful, smooth tapestry fabric.

Brocaded effects are achieved by varying the size of the stitches to produce a texture and sheen that resembles satin brocade. At first this appears to be very difficult but one soon discovers that the thread count is repeated in one row above another, or in an arrangement of two short stitches above two long stitches as in the pattern copied from the actual Bargello design reproduced in the photograph on page 64. Some brocade textures are created by sewing three small stitches above one long one as seen in Brocade Stripes on page 24. There are many variations which you may develop on your own as your enthusiasm increases.

While I urge all beginners to choose a simple zigzag or any other easy pattern for their first piece, I realize that the creative individual will find more challenge in trying a complicated motif. To solve the rhythmical repeat of a pattern and at the same time create a colorful blending of tones is a most enjoyable and satisfying experience.

In addition to canvas and tapestry yarns, a few Number 22 tapestry needles are all the equipment that is required to begin these designs. Hoops and frames are not necessary since all threads will be arranged in one direction.

It is best to begin most designs in the middle of the canvas area which will permit one to decide how far to extend the pattern either horizontally or vertically. For example: when working a large pattern for a chair seat or a pillow, it is important to center the motif and this can easily be arranged when you have begun your work in the middle of the canvas area.

It is not advisable to cut strands of tapestry yarn into one standard length as is customary in working monotone needle-point backgrounds. Since Bargello designs vary the amount of each color, it is more practical to cut the yarn as it is needed from a continuous skein. For large areas, it is best to limit the thread length to 24 inches.

The completed piece should be pressed flat by laying the right side of the embroidery on a smooth, padded surface. A wet pressing cloth and a dry iron will produce better results than a temperamental steam iron.

There is a most important word of caution which I cannot emphasize enough for those who are attempting Bargello Embroidery for the first time. When working with tapestry yarn it is essential to keep the wool thread soft and relaxed. Should the canvas weave show between the yarn, you are pulling your stitches too tightly or you may be twisting the thread. The entire surface of the finished piece should be covered with smooth, evenly-spaced stitches in softly blending shades of the yarn colors.

All the designs in this book were worked on square weave, mono-thread canvas containing thirteen threads-per-inch. The tapestry yarn was developed by the author and is stocked in fine needlework shops. If the reader is unable to obtain any of these materials, information is available from Needlecraft House, West Townsend, Massachusetts.

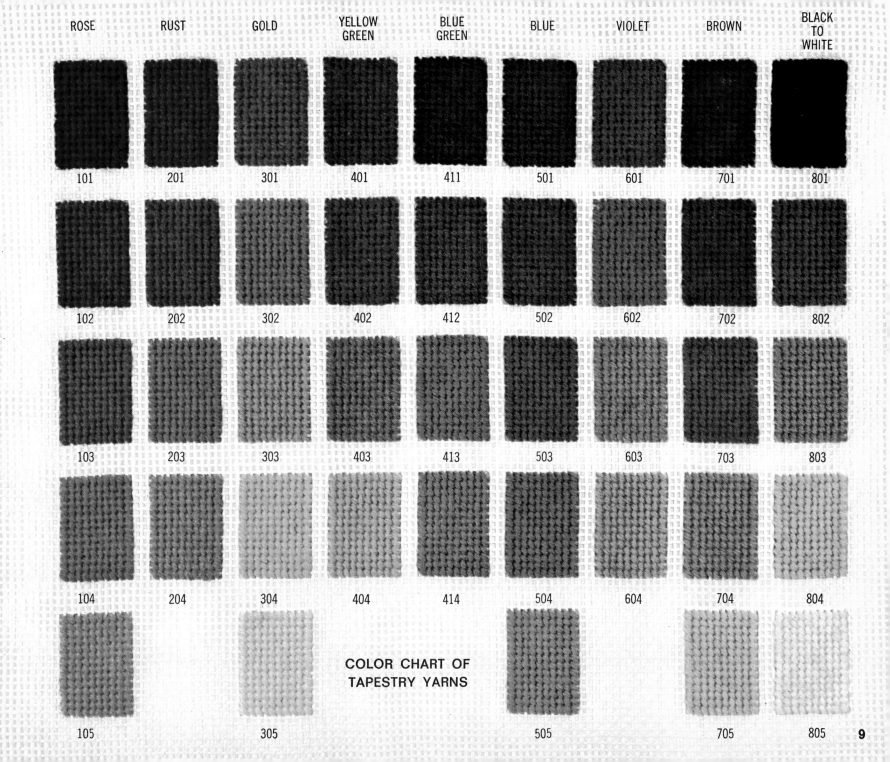

COLOR CHART OF
TAPESTRY YARNS

9

BASKET WEAVE

The pattern is created with parallel stitches advancing in a diagonal row. Each row contains 8 pairs of stitches. The bands in one direction are worked in 4 shades of yellow-green. The bands crossing them are in 4 shades of blue. Four pairs of black stitches form the small squares. All stitches are over 4 threads of canvas.

401	Yellow-Green
402	Yellow-Green
403	Yellow-Green
404	Yellow-Green
502	Blue
503	Blue
504	Blue
505	Blue
801	Black

INTERLOCKING BANDS

This design would make beautiful window valances. It requires three colors against a neutral background. The gray shadow across the bottom of the border creates a three-dimensional effect. All stitches are over 4 and under 2 canvas threads.

102	Rose
103	Rose
104	Rose
105	Rose
301	Gold
302	Gold
303	Gold
304	Gold
502	Blue
503	Blue
504	Blue
505	Blue
801	Black
802	Gray
803	Gray
804	Gray

SHADOWED SQUARES

The blue shadows of this design create an interesting dimensional effect. All stitches are worked in pairs and are sewn over 4 threads. The design is excellent for rugs and upholstery.

101   Rose

501   Blue

804   Gray

FISH SCALE

A lovely old pattern of small proportions which can be applied to a project of any size. The colors are arranged to begin with a small center of deep yellow gold 302. Most stitches are over 4 threads, but a few at the side are over 2 or 6 to adjust to the curve. This design is also called: Eye of the Peacock.

302   Gold
303   Gold
304   Gold

603   Violet
602   Violet

503   Blue
502   Blue
501   Blue

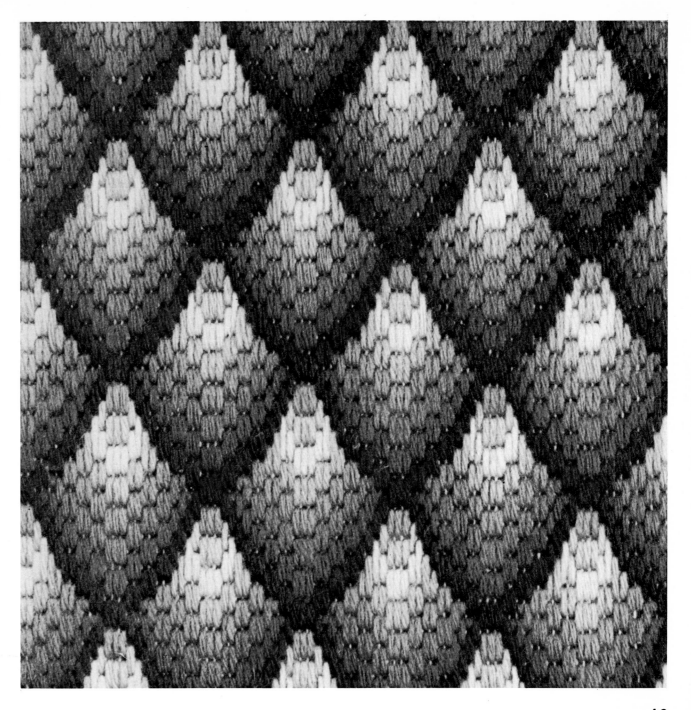

PINK TULIPS

Two shades of green form the leaves and two shades of rose are used in the tulips with white as a background. All stitches are sewn over 4 threads. Lavender tulips also combine well against a light blue background.

805 White

411 Blue-Green
412 Blue-Green

102 Rose
103 Rose

ZIGZAG

This is the easiest pattern of all. Four shades of green are followed by four shades of blue, working only one row of each shade at a time, repeating the two sets of color. All stitches are worked over 4 threads of canvas.

411 Blue-Green
412 Blue-Green
413 Blue-Green
414 Blue-Green

501 Blue
502 Blue
503 Blue
504 Blue

DIMENSIONAL DIAMONDS

Worked in shades of one color, this simple pattern will not conflict with nearby surface embroidery designs. All stitches are worked over 4 threads. It would be effective worked in four shades of any color.

701   Brown
703   Brown
704   Brown
705   Brown

CORDUROY SQUARES

This modern design is worked in black, gray, and white against a colored background. All stitches cover 4 threads and are sewn in even rows to create the corduroy effect. A gold background was used in the original, however, the pattern is effective against any color.

801   Black

804   Gray

805   White

302   Gold

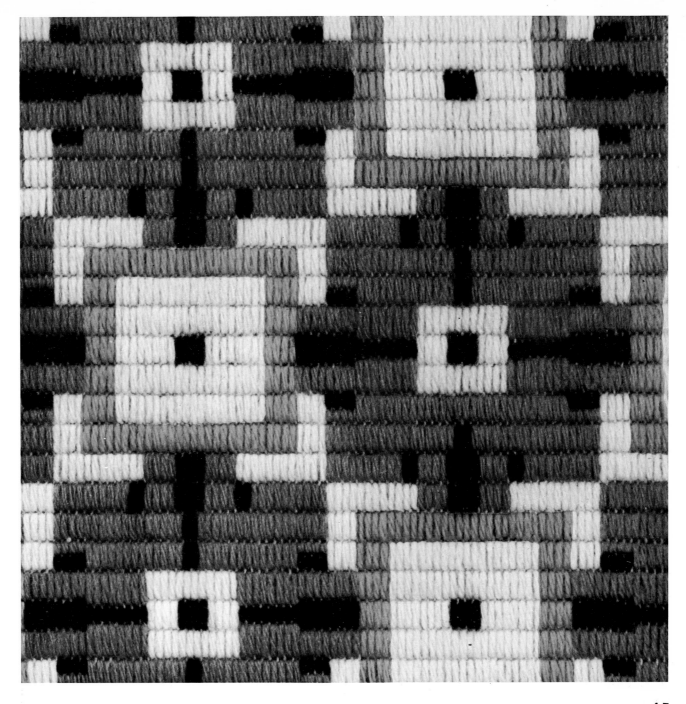

FIAMMA SEMPLICE

Here is a simplified form of Flame Stitch. Work all stitches over 4 threads beginning with a zigzag row of brown. Four stitches of gold 302 are sewn above the lower points of brown. Continue upward, sewing one row each of 4 shades of rust. A row of gold 303 follows, omitting the top stitch of the low peak to insert another four stitches of gold 302. Continue upward using 4 shades of yellow-green with a final row of gold 303.

701   Brown

302   Gold
303   Gold

201   Rust
202   Rust
203   Rust
204   Rust

401   Yellow-Green
402   Yellow-Green
403   Yellow-Green
404   Yellow-Green

SWEDISH DIAMONDS

Four shades of blue with white produce this simple diamond pattern which is frequently seen in Scandinavian embroideries. A row of white zigzag will quickly establish the pattern.

805   White

501   Blue
502   Blue
503   Blue
504   Blue

HUNGARIAN BORDER

A smooth, satin effect is achieved with parallel stitches in the solid border. All other stitches are worked in pairs to create the texture of the design. It would make a beautiful table cover or square pillow. The center, solid area is worked in gold 303 with all stitches sewn over 4 threads except at the edge where smaller stitches, over 2 threads, meet the dark border. The design in gold 301 has 2, 4, 6, and 8 thread stitches. The background of the border design is 304.

301 Gold
303 Gold
304 Gold

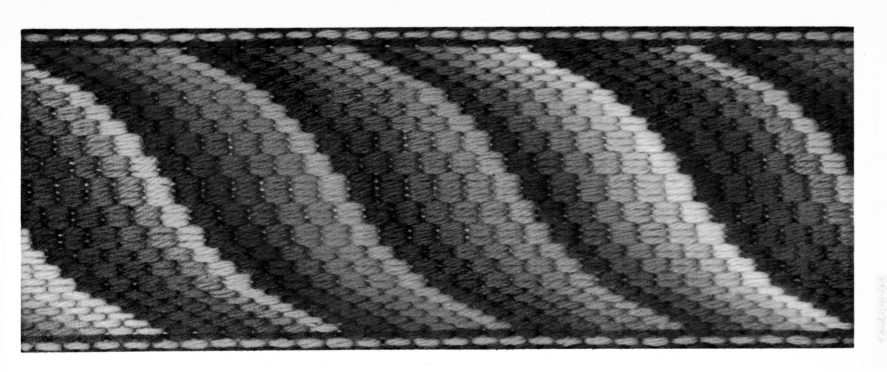

SPIRAL BANDS

This beautiful band of colors could be used as a bell pull or as an edging on draperies. It has unlimited application for small items such as desk blotters, waste baskets, and box bands.

101	Rose	501	Blue	301	Gold	401	Yellow-Green
102	Rose	502	Blue	302	Gold	402	Yellow-Green
103	Rose	503	Blue	303	Gold	403	Yellow-Green
104	Rose	504	Blue	304	Gold	404	Yellow-Green
105	Rose	505	Blue	305	Gold		
						701	Brown

LOLLYPOP TREES

This fascinating pattern can be worked in four shades of one color alone to obtain a damask effect, or in two colors, alternating the rows, to create horizontal stripes. All stitches are sewn over 4 threads of the canvas.

501	Blue
502	Blue
503	Blue
504	Blue
301	Gold
302	Gold
303	Gold
304	Gold
101	Rose
102	Rose
103	Rose
104	Rose
401	Yellow-Green
402	Yellow-Green
403	Yellow-Green
404	Yellow-Green

TWIN DIAMONDS

The diamonds in this design may be repeated in additional rows above and below. Five shades of one color are needed to complete the design and all stitches are sewn over 4 threads of the canvas.

101   Rose
102   Rose
103   Rose
104   Rose
105   Rose

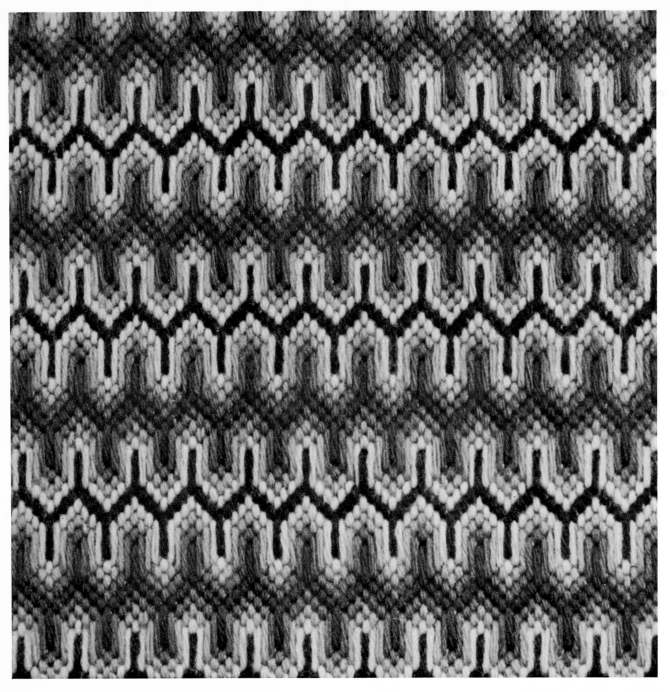

BROCADE STRIPES

The brocaded texture of this pattern is achieved by varying the size of the stitches. All the small stitches are sewn over 2 threads of canvas. The long stitches are sewn over 6 threads. Establish the pattern in dark-brown 701. Continue with one row each of 705, 704, 703, 702, 703, 704, 705. Repeat, beginning again with 701.

701   Brown
702   Brown
703   Brown
704   Brown
705   Brown

MAGIC LANTERN

Five shades of blue create
the light motif with the
lightest shade at the edge of
the design. Five shades of rose
make the shadowed pattern
with the darkest shade at
the outer edge. The short
stitches cover 4 canvas
threads; long stitches cover
8 canvas threads.

101	Rose
102	Rose
103	Rose
104	Rose
105	Rose
501	Blue
502	Blue
503	Blue
504	Blue
505	Blue

DIAMOND BROCADE

This design requires careful concentration as to the length of the stitches which develop the brocaded texture. Small stitches are worked over 2 threads of canvas. Long stitches are worked over 4 threads of canvas. The design is most effective in black, grays, and white, but may be worked in 5 shades of one color. Beginning with an outline of black 801, work toward the center with one row each of 802, 803, 804, 805, 804, 803. Four small stitches of 802 are the center of each motif.

801	Black
802	Gray
803	Gray
804	Gray
805	White

SHADOWED MESH

The zigzag rows of light-gold are sewn over 4 threads of canvas. The squares formed between these lines are then filled with two shades of gold. The first stitch is over 2 threads, the second over 4; the third over 6, and the fourth again over 4. Repeat remaining half of the square from the opposite side.

301   Gold
303   Gold
305   Gold

SATIN FLAME

Two rows of the darkest shade create the deep contrasting tones of this flame. Three rows each of a lighter shade, complete the motif. Arrange rust shades below the brown, and green shades above the brown, with lightest shades at the top of each flame. All stitches are sewn over 4 threads of canvas.

701 Brown
702 Brown
703 Brown
704 Brown

401 Yellow-Green
402 Yellow-Green
403 Yellow-Green
404 Yellow-Green

201 Rust
202 Rust
203 Rust
204 Rust

CHAIN MAIL

Four shades of green and one row of light-gray were used to make this design but it can also be worked in five shades of one color. All stitches are worked over 4 threads of canvas.

411   Blue-Green
412   Blue-Green
413   Blue-Green
414   Blue-Green

804   Gray

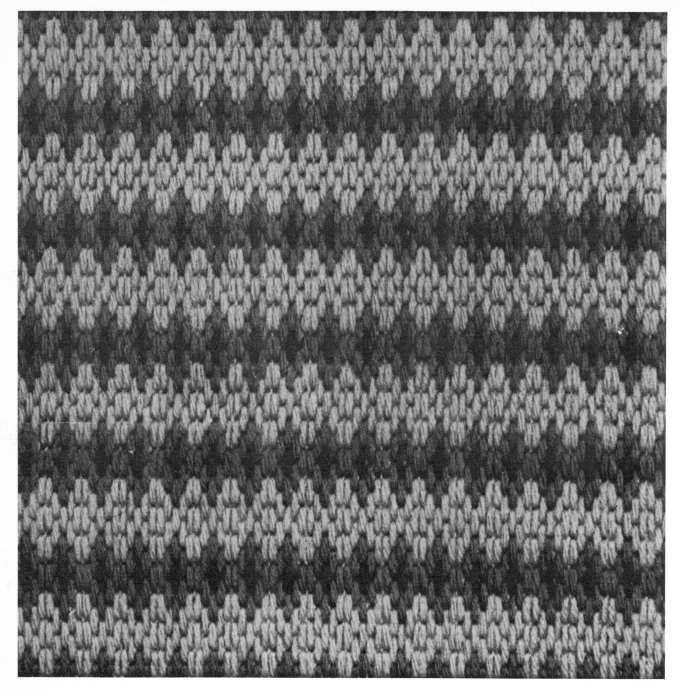

DUO TONES

The lighter stripe is worked in one tone of the lightest shade, but the dark row has a darker stitch in the center of each diamond. All stitches are sewn over 4 threads of canvas.

501 Blue
503 Blue
505 Blue

FLORAL MEDALLION

A beautiful design that suggests many possible ways of combining the emphasis of needlepoint with Bargello canvas work. The pattern was adapted from an embroidery by Louise A. Chrimes.

401	Yellow-Green
402	Yellow-Green
403	Yellow-Green
404	Yellow-Green
302	Gold
303	Gold
304	Gold

Needlepoint Center

804	Gray (background)
101	Rose (flowers)
104	Rose
105	Rose

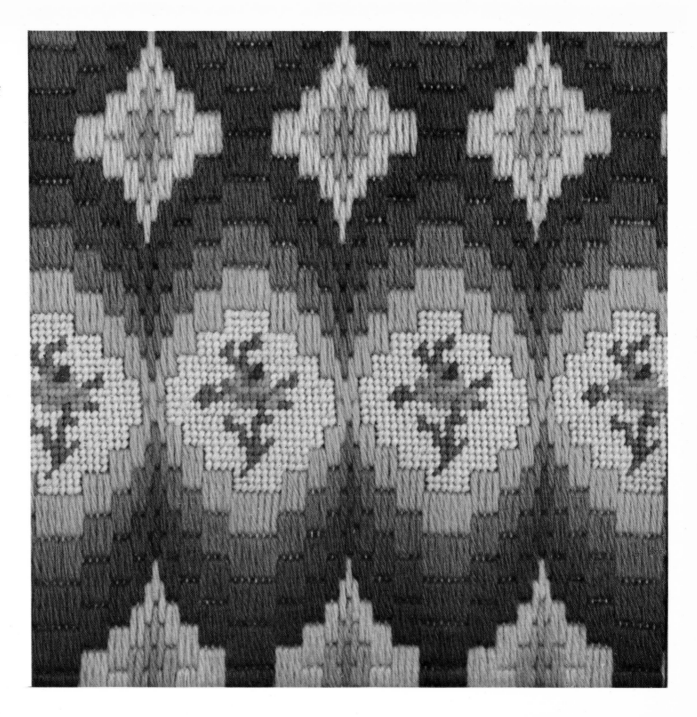

TIFFANY TULIP

The black outline of the flower produces the stained-glass effect which appears to illuminate the tulips. This striking design is excellent for upholstery and cushions. All stitches are sewn over 4 threads of canvas.

801   Black

301   Gold
304   Gold
305   Gold

403   Yellow-Green
404   Yellow-Green

KELIM MEDALLION

This handsome repeat would develop into an elegant canvas-worked rug. The design could be arranged to fit any size but it would need a plain border to frame the edges.

411   Blue-Green

503   Blue

401   Yellow-Green
403   Yellow-Green

705   Brown

AURORA BOREALIS

This is a very easy pattern to follow once the first row is established. The effect is produced chiefly by the choice of colors which blend into each other creating this beautiful mirage. All stitches are sewn over 4 threads of canvas.

502	Blue
503	Blue
504	Blue
505	Blue
601	Violet
602	Violet
603	Violet
604	Violet
102	Rose
103	Rose
104	Rose
105	Rose

LIGHTED DIAMONDS

This design is a fascinating one because the diamonds appear to be illuminated by the three light-gold stitches at the top of each peak. Alternate rows of green diamonds with rows of gold diamonds. All stitches are sewn over 4 canvas threads.

401   Yellow-Green
402   Yellow-Green
403   Yellow-Green
404   Yellow-Green

301   Gold
302   Gold
303   Gold
304   Gold
305   Gold

DOMES AND SPIRES

This old Florentine pattern may have been inspired by the dome of the Baptistery. Six rows of tones are created by using five shades of blue and one of black. All stitches are sewn over 4 threads of canvas.

801   Black

501   Blue
502   Blue
503   Blue
504   Blue
505   Blue

SEAMED SQUARES

The texture created by the seams makes this an unusual pattern. All stitches are arranged in pairs and sewn over 4 threads of canvas except where smaller stitches are required to maintain the seam line. These smaller stitches are worked over 2 threads. The rust centers are surrounded by rows of tan and medium-brown, with dark-brown edges.

202   Rust

701   Brown
703   Brown
705   Brown

FLINT ARROWS

Beginning with black and graduating to white, the pattern includes three shades of gray. The white center is balanced by gray tones until it again returns to the black. This unusual design must be worked over 6 threads of canvas to create the tall, arrowed streaks and the dynamic movement of the design.

801 Black

802 Gray
803 Gray
804 Gray

805 White

BYZANTINE TURRETS

A strong pattern is achieved by the sharp contrast of white against black. An arrangement of gray occurs in some of the turrets to add interest to the pattern. All stitches are worked over 4 threads of canvas.

801   Black

802   Gray

805   White

CHEVRONS

Remindful of military merit ribbons, these chevrons of rose, light-gray 804 and deep-blue are worked over 4 threads of canvas. The spaces between each completed chevron are worked with smaller stitches covering 2 threads of canvas. A shadow beneath the blue chevron is achieved by working one row of dark-gray 802.

101	Rose
501	Blue
802	Gray
803	Gray
804	Gray

SERRATA

This vibrant pattern requires five shades of a color for each layer of serrated points. The first row of the darkest shade is worked with each stitch covering 8 threads of canvas. The second row requires a four-thread stitch at the peak to flatten the top. The third row has 3 four-thread stitches at the top. The peak of the fourth row has 2 four-thread, 1 eight-thread, plus 2 four-thread stitches. The last row adjusts to fit the previous row and prepares you for the pale-gray points.

501	Blue
502	Blue
503	Blue
504	Blue
505	Blue
101	Rose
102	Rose
103	Rose
104	Rose
105	Rose
804	Gray

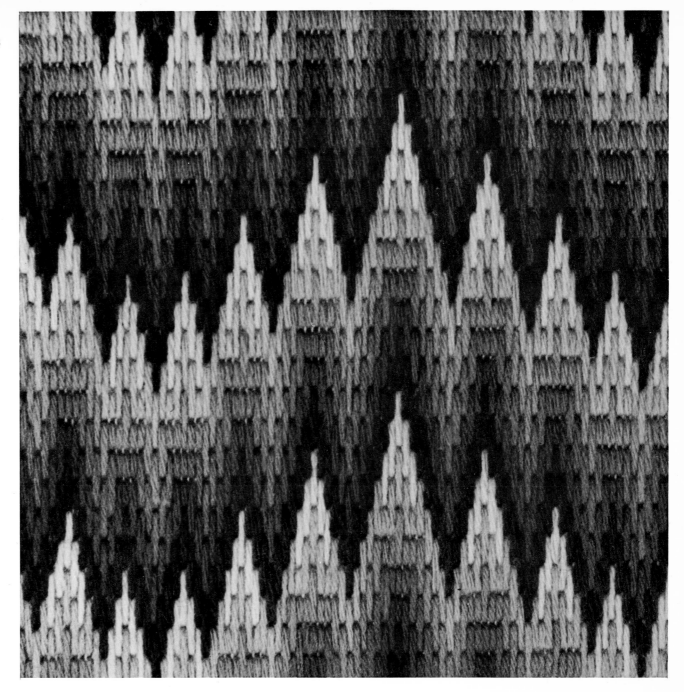

FUSED DIAMONDS

This design requires 6 tones of color plus an outline of black. Working up from the lower black line it uses 2 rows each of four rust shades followed by 3 rows of brown 704 topped with a center diamond of light-brown 705. All stitches are worked over 4 threads of canvas.

201   Rust
202   Rust
203   Rust
204   Rust

704   Brown
705   Brown

801   Black

SATIN RIPPLES

This unusual pattern is worked with stitches sewn over 2 threads and over 6 threads of canvas. The possible combinations of colors are endless since this design can be worked either in graduations of one color or in contrasting tones.

502	Blue
503	Blue
804	Gray
302	Gold
305	Gold
404	Yellow-Green

POMEGRANATE

One of the oldest patterns, this is frequently found in Early American collections. It has been used for purses, pillows, and chair seats, but would also be excellent for small rugs.

Blue Scrolls
801   Black

501   Blue
502   Blue
503   Blue
504   Blue
505   Blue

Center Diamonds
101   Rose
102   Rose

DIABOLO

Fine for a centered design this pattern is worked with the motif positioned as shown although the finished piece is also attractive when applied sideways. A beautiful damask effect is achieved when this pattern is embroidered in five shades of one color. All stitches are worked over 4 threads of canvas.

501   Blue
502   Blue
503   Blue
504   Blue
505   Blue

DEEP BOXES

The three-dimensional
effect of this design is
amazing. At the base of the
boxes a black square
increases the depth which is
created by using five shades
of one color. All stitches
are arranged in pairs and
worked over 4 threads of
canvas. A smaller design can
be formed with three shades
of a color against a small
black square.

101   Rose
102   Rose
103   Rose
104   Rose
105   Rose

801   Black

LATTICE

Five shades of a color plus black form the lattice boards which appear to be rounded. The shadow of the gray background increases the three-dimensional effect. All stitches are worked over 4 threads of canvas.

101	Rose
102	Rose
103	Rose
104	Rose
105	Rose
801	Black
802	Gray
803	Gray
804	Gray

MITRED SQUARES

The center stitch at the middle of this mitre is over 4 threads. All other stitches are sewn over 3 threads of canvas. Gray was used for the two center cross rows. Five shades of rose next are followed by one gray, then 5 more lines of the rose shades, plus 1 gray, etc.

101	Rose
102	Rose
103	Rose
104	Rose
105	Rose
802	Gray

HEARTS AND DIAMONDS

Five shades of one color form this beautiful brocaded effect. If the diamonds are worked in contrasting color tones to silhouette the heart shape, this design is then called "Overlapping Pomegranates." All stitches are worked over 4 threads of canvas.

501 Blue
502 Blue
503 Blue
504 Blue
505 Blue

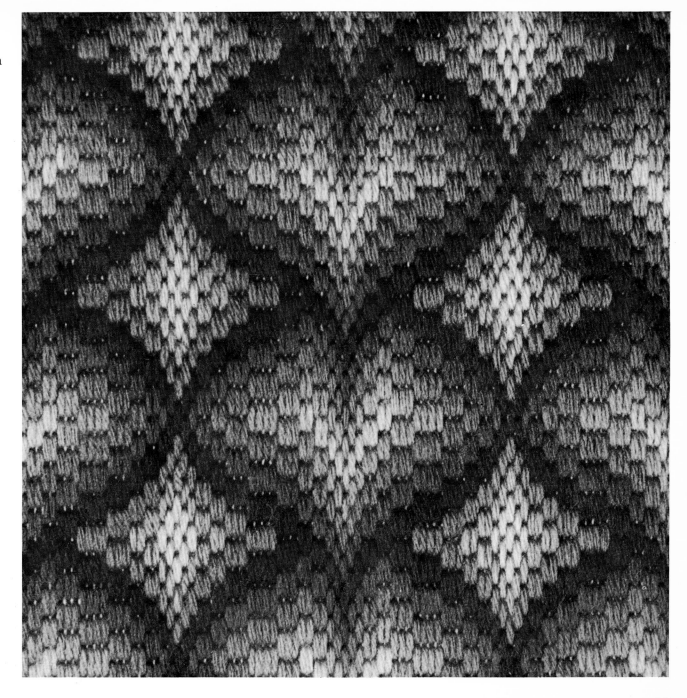

CORAL FANS

Begin the pattern at the lowest point using rust 201 and proceed upward using 202, 203, 204, 301, 302, 303, 304. Brown 701 creates the outside line of the pattern. All stitches are sewn over 4 threads of canvas.

201   Rust
202   Rust
203   Rust
204   Rust

301   Gold
302   Gold
303   Gold
304   Gold

701   Brown

REFLECTIONS

This striking design requires careful attention in counting the canvas threads. The light yellow-green background is a repeat of stitches over 2-4-6-4-2 threads. The design forming the blue reflections is worked over 2 and 6 threads creating a brocaded effect. Notice that there are always two rows of stitches sewn over 6 threads followed by two rows of stitches sewn over 2 threads of canvas.

501   Blue
502   Blue
503   Blue
504   Blue
505   Blue

404   Yellow-Green

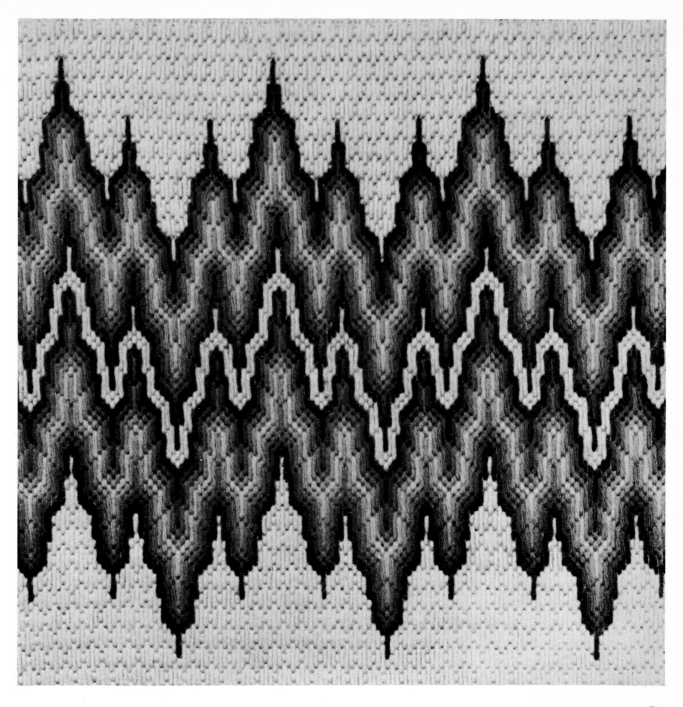

DIMINISHING DIAMONDS

Four shades of brown and four shades of gold diminish into points of light-brown. This is an easy-to-follow pattern and could be used on many small items. It is worked with all stitches over 4 threads of canvas.

701 Brown
702 Brown
703 Brown
704 Brown
705 Brown

301 Gold
302 Gold
303 Gold
304 Gold

IVY
LEAVES

Used as a border, for luggage racks or desk blotters this can be very attractive but it is especially handsome when worked in stripes for chair seats and upholstery.

411 Blue-Green
412 Blue-Green
413 Blue-Green

403 Yellow-Green
404 Yellow-Green

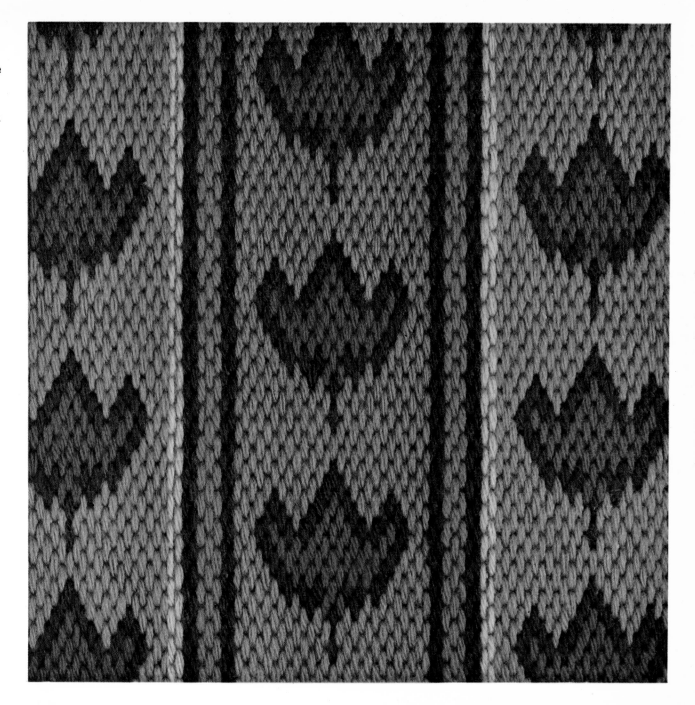

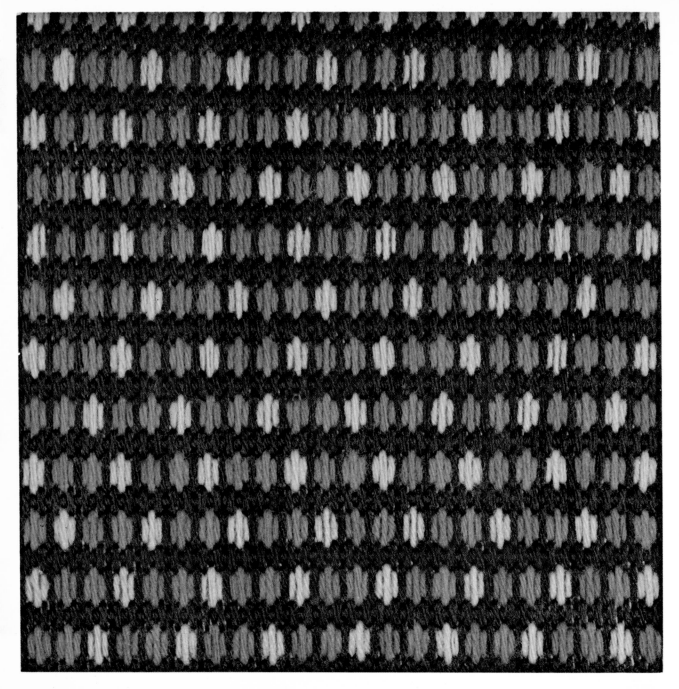

MULTI GEMS

The repeat of three colors against a dull background causes this design to sparkle. It is excellent for many small projects. The stitches of the colored diamonds are sewn over 4 and 6 threads of canvas.

411 Blue-Green

304 Gold

104 Rose

504 Blue

DIAMOND GEMS

The rose and pink center stitches add luster to the diamonds of this interesting arrangement. All stitches are sewn over 4 threads of canvas.

102   Rose
104   Rose

501   Blue
503   Blue
504   Blue
505   Blue

412   Blue-Green
414   Blue-Green

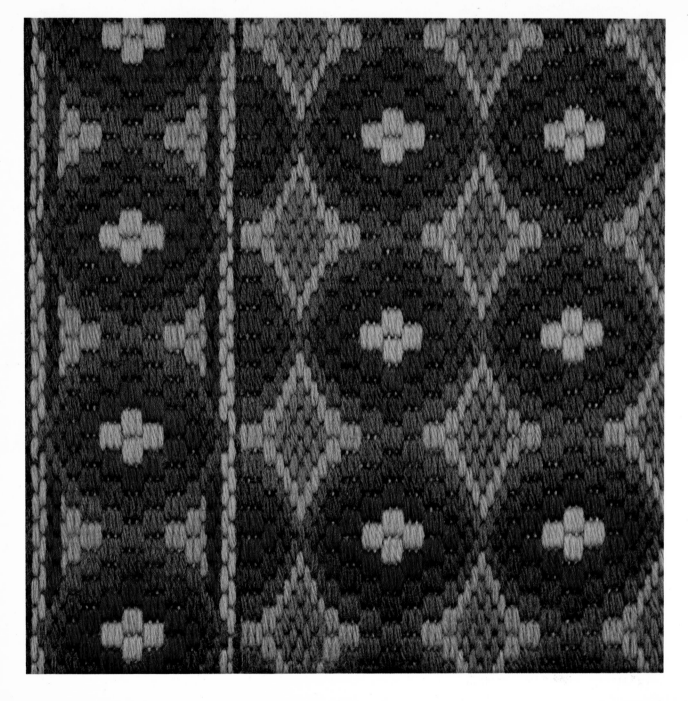

PERSIAN BORDER

A handsome old pattern
which can be used with or
without the border. The
border stripe by itself is
excellent for making luggage
straps or ribbon bands. All
stitches are over 4 threads.
The center area of this motif
without the border is
attractive as an overall
design.

501   Blue

101   Rose

412   Blue-Green

303   Gold

802   Gray
803   Gray

HUNGARIAN RHAPSODY

Establish the pattern with dark-blue 501 and continue working upward above the blue line with rows of stitches arranged in the following order: 1 row—301, 1 row—704, 1 row—705, 1 row—303, 2 rows—403, 2 rows—401, 1 row—303, 1 row—704, 1 row—505, 1 row—503. All stitches are worked over 4 threads of canvas.

501   Blue
503   Blue
505   Blue

301   Gold
303   Gold

704   Brown
705   Brown

401   Yellow-Green
403   Yellow-Green

DIAMOND BANDS

The horizontal stitches of the gold stripes create a satin texture in contrast to the remaining area of stitches sewn vertically over 4 threads of canvas. The centers of the diamonds and the middle of the gold stripes are rose. A black background surrounds the diamonds.

303   Gold

101   Rose

801   Black

(Adapted from a sampler by A. Karn, 1847. Courtesy of The Embroiderers' Guild, London, England.)

JEWELED HEXAGONS

This vertical hexagonal form is achieved by using one row of gold—301, one row—302, two rows—303, two rows—304, one row—305, with a black outline around each form. All stitches are worked over 4 threads of canvas.

301   Gold
302   Gold
303   Gold
304   Gold
305   Gold

801   Black

(Adapted from a sampler by A. Karn, 1847. Courtesy of The Embroiderers' Guild, London, England.)

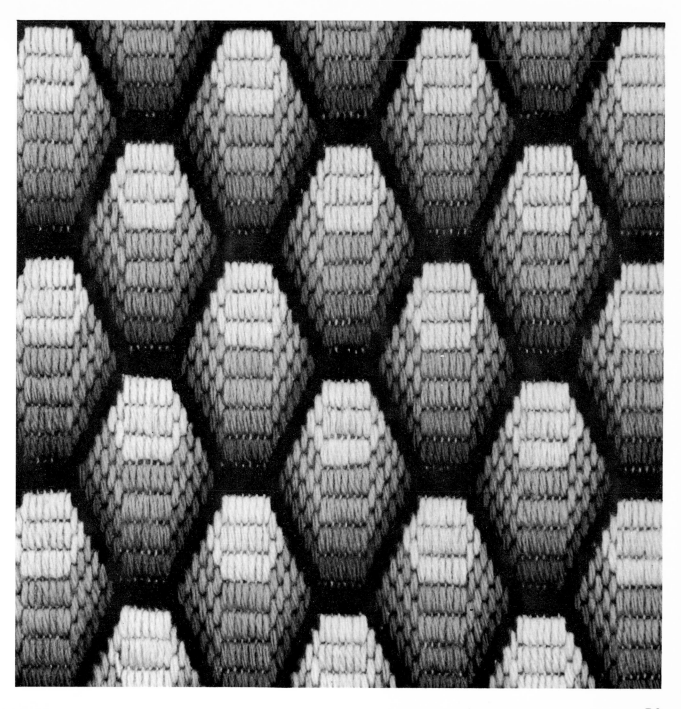

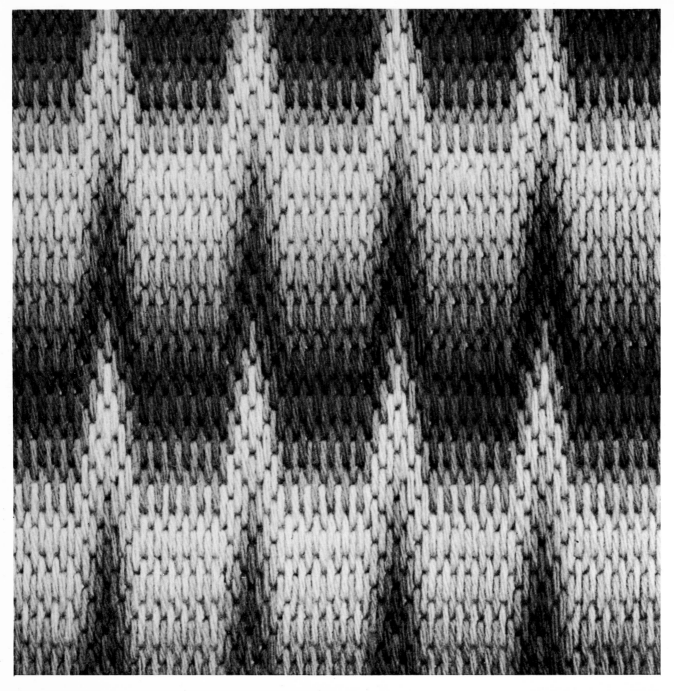

FLORENTINE RHYTHMS

Establish the pattern with the darkest shade of yellow-green 401. Continue working other green shades toward the lower part of the design ending in lightest-green 404. Embroider the darkest shade of violet above the darkest green and continue working upward to the lightest violet. All stitches are sewn over 4 threads of canvas.

401   Yellow-Green
402   Yellow-Green
403   Yellow-Green
404   Yellow-Green

601   Violet
602   Violet
603   Violet
604   Violet

ETERNAL WAVES

Establish the pattern with
the row of white stitches.
Graduate from light to dark
with rows of rose below the
white line and rows of blue
above the white line. The row
of darkest blue has dark
rose next to it. All stitches
are sewn over 4 threads of
canvas.

805　White

101　Rose
102　Rose
103　Rose
104　Rose
105　Rose

501　Blue
502　Blue
503　Blue
504　Blue
505　Blue

*(Adapted from a pillow top.
Courtesy of the Victoria
and Albert Museum, London,
England.)*

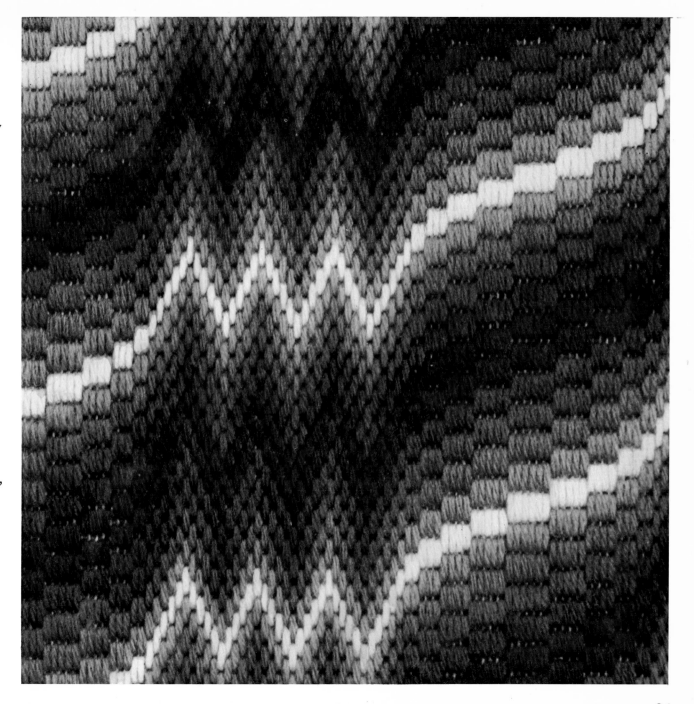

FLORENTINE DAMASK

Since the size of stitches varies constantly, this design requires careful attention to the canvas thread-count. It includes 2-4-6-8-10 and 12-thread stitches. The light arrow motif is worked in brown 704. The darkest area forming most of the design is in blue-green 413. Rust 203 is worked in 23 flat stitches adjacent to the arrow form and in the diamond and dot forms that appear in the middle of the green. The outline form of the remaining motifs is worked in brown 703.

413 Blue-Green

203 Rust

703 Brown
704 Brown

TRADITIONAL CARNATIONS

This design is worked with stitches over 4 threads of canvas. Outline entire pattern in green 404. Beginning at the inside of the base of this outline, work another single row outline in green 403 to form the calyx. All the remaining area of flower and calyx is worked in shades of blue. Background of the design is in rust.

201 Rust

403 Yellow-Green
404 Yellow-Green

501 Blue
503 Blue
504 Blue
505 Blue

(Adapted from an original piece at The Embroiderers' Guild, London, England. Gift of Miss Joan Alexander.)

BARGELLO

This historic pattern, originally worked in silk, may be seen on 17th-century chairs at the Bargello Museum in Florence, Italy. The brocade is worked with 2 rows sewn over 6 threads of canvas followed by two rows over 2 threads. Repeat these 4 rows of canvas thread-count. With colors arranged in the following order begin the design with dark-blue 501 at the bottom edge of the narrow border and work upward.

1 Row 501
2 Rows 303
1 Row 501
2 Rows 805
2 Rows 305
2 Rows 403
2 Rows 413
1 Row 411
1 Row 305
2 Rows 805
1 Row 305
1 Row 411
2 Rows 413
2 Rows 403
2 Rows 305
2 Rows 805
and repeat.

(Adapted from 17th-century chairs in the Museo Nazionale, Florence, Italy.)